First World War
and Army of Occupation
War Diary
France, Belgium and Germany

27 DIVISION
Divisional Troops
Divisional Ammunition Column
21 December 1914 - 1 January 1916

WO95/2257/7

The Naval & Military Press Ltd
www.nmarchive.com
Published in association with The National Archives

Published by

The Naval & Military Press Ltd

Unit 10 Ridgewood Industrial Park,

Uckfield, East Sussex,

TN22 5QE England

Tel: +44 (0) 1825 749494

www.naval-military-press.com

www.nmarchive.com

This diary has been reprinted in facsimile from the original. Any imperfections are inevitably reproduced and the quality may fall short of modern type and cartographic standards.

© **Crown Copyright**
Images reproduced by permission of The National Archives, London, England, 2015.

Contents

Document type	Place/Title	Date From	Date To
Heading	WO95/2257/7		
Heading	27th Division Divl Artillery 27th Divl Ammn Column Dec 1914-Dec 1915		
Heading	27th Divn Ammn Col 21/12/14-Dec 1915		
Heading	27th Divisional Ammun Coln Vol I 21.12.14-28.2.15		
War Diary	Slough	21/12/1914	21/12/1914
War Diary	Le Havre	22/12/1914	23/12/1914
War Diary	Aire & Wittes	25/12/1914	25/12/1914
War Diary	Wittes	27/12/1914	27/12/1914
War Diary	Borre	07/01/1915	07/01/1915
War Diary	Reninghelst	08/01/1915	12/01/1915
War Diary	Boeschepe	13/01/1915	28/02/1915
Heading	27th Divl Ammn Coln Vol II 1-25.3.15		
War Diary	Boeschepe	01/03/1915	25/03/1915
Heading	27th Divl Ammun Coln Vol III 1-30.4.15		
War Diary	Boeschepe	01/04/1915	05/04/1915
War Diary	Poperinghe	07/04/1915	24/04/1915
War Diary	Vlamertinghe	25/04/1915	27/04/1915
War Diary	Near Vlamertinghe	28/04/1915	30/04/1915
Heading	27th Division 27th Divl. Ammun Coln Vol IV 1-31.5.15		
War Diary	Sheet 28 Farm G.21.C.	01/05/1915	03/05/1915
War Diary	G. 26. C.	08/05/1915	31/05/1915
War Diary	Sheet 36 B. 27. C.	31/05/1915	31/05/1915
Heading	27th Division 27th Divl. Ammun. Coln Vol V June 1915		
War Diary	Pepinette	01/06/1915	15/06/1915
Heading	27th Division 27th Divl. Ammun Coln Vol VI		
War Diary	Bivouack At L'Hall 'O' Beau Nr. Armontieres	01/07/1915	01/07/1915
War Diary	La Sequemeau	15/07/1915	15/07/1915
War Diary	Froid Nid.	24/07/1915	24/07/1915
Heading	27th Division 27th Ammunition Col Aug-Oct. 15 Vol VII		
War Diary	Bivouack Near Steenwerck	01/08/1915	31/08/1915
War Diary	Bivouack Near Steenwerck	06/09/1915	09/09/1915
War Diary	Steen-Je	14/09/1915	20/09/1915
War Diary	Blangy	21/09/1915	24/09/1915
War Diary	Hamelet	25/09/1915	25/09/1915
War Diary	Hamel.	04/10/1915	23/10/1915
War Diary	Boves	24/10/1915	25/10/1915
War Diary	Breilly	25/10/1915	25/10/1915
Heading	27th Div. Ammun. Col. Nov. 1915 Vol VIII		
War Diary	In The Field	01/11/1915	30/11/1915
Heading	27 Divl Ammun. Col. Dec Vol. IX		
War Diary		01/12/1915	31/12/1915
War Diary	In Action	16/12/1915	16/12/1915
War Diary	In The Field	01/01/1916	01/01/1916
Heading	G S 217 Personnel Ammn Column		
Miscellaneous	Head Quarters, 27th Division	11/01/1915	11/01/1915
Miscellaneous			

W095/22514

27TH DIVISION
DIVL ARTILLERY

27TH DIVL AMMN COLUMN
DEC 1914 - DEC 1915

27th Divn
Ammn Col
21/12/14 – Dec 1915

121/4586

27th Divisional Ammⁿ Colⁿ

Vol I 21.12.14 — 28.2.15

Nil

XXVIIth DIVNL AMMN COL.

WAR DIARY
or
INTELLIGENCE SUMMARY
(Erase heading not required.)

Army Form C. 2118.

Instructions regarding War Diaries and Intelligence Summaries are contained in F. S. Regs., Part II. and the Staff Manual respectively. Title pages will be prepared in manuscript.

Hour, Date, Place	Summary of Events and Information	Remarks and references to Appendices
Dec. 21st 1914 – SLOUGH	Column entrained in 6 trains for Southampton; embarked in S.S. "Archimedes" for LE HAVRE. Strength: 14 officers 395 O.R. / 1st train 22-23-	440 horses.
Dec. 22nd 7/9/14 LE HAVRE	Disembarked. Bivouacked in Dockside till midnight 22-23-	
" 23rd " "	Entrained 1st train GARE DES MARCHANDISES – 12.20 am 23-24th. 2nd train at 7 hours interval after	
" 25th " AIRE	1st train arrived at AIRE 12.20 am. 2nd at AIRE CQUES – 5 am –	
" " 9 WITTES	3rd " " " 11.2.30 pm – Each detail marching to WITTES; there to be billeted.	
Dec. 27th 1914 – WITTES	2/Lieut A.C. Buckell reported for duty from 1st Bde Amn Col R.F.A.	
Dec. Jan. 7th 1915. BORRE	Left WITTES at 9.30 am. for BORRE via HAZEBROUCK. 10 miles. Left V.O. & 15 men with sick horses.	
Jan. 8th. 1915. RENINGHELST	Marched on RENINGHELST, there to be billeted. 1st Section 5th Divl Amn Col. reported/joined here to supply XVth Bde R.F.A.	
Jan 12th " "	2/Lt Buckell & party to WITTES to fetch sick horses now convalescent.	
Jan 13th " BOESCHEPE	Moved by road to BOESCHEPE – Here to be billeted	
Jan 19th " "	Party to CAESTRE for remounts 1st Batteries. 42 horses brought in next day.	
Jan 26th " "	Stampede of horses due to undiscovered cause.	
Jan 25th " "	Court of Inquiry re Stampede. No finding.	
Jan 27th " "	10 NCOs & men reported sick – hors – 1st Bde R.F.A.	
Jan 29th " "	2/Lieut D. May left for England made Steele.	
Feby 15th " "	over 7000 rds 18 pr Shrapnel issued, in the occasion of the German attack near hillocks.	
" 16th " "	34 mules brought in Sunday aft.	
" 17th " "	Right section moved to G. 36.a. near OUDERDOM. Trucks to be billeted	
" 19th " "	99 horses drawn from GODEWAERSVELDE for Amn Coly.	
" 28th " "	94 mules drawn from " " Militia of 1.B. less horses to Column	

LIEUT.COL.
AMN. COL
COMMANDING XXVIIth DIVNL AMN. COL

121/5320

27th Dio Numen Ch

Intten 1 — 25.3.15

Army Form C. 2118.

WAR DIARY
or
INTELLIGENCE SUMMARY
(Erase heading not required.)

Hour, Date, Place	Summary of Events and Information	Remarks and references to Appendices
March 1st Boeschepe	} nothing to report	
March 8th		
March 13th–14th "	13000 res gun ammun. sent out to Brigades in consequence of punishing attack amm. stored position.	
March 23rd "	Column inspected by G.O.C. VIIth Corps.	
March 25th "	No 1. (advanced) section moved back from OUDERDOM.	

[signature]

LIEUT.-COL.,
COMMANDING XXVIIth DIVNL. AMN. COL.

121/5408

27th Air Armn Coy
Vol 116 1 - 30.4.45

WAR DIARY
or
INTELLIGENCE SUMMARY
(Erase heading not required.)

Army Form C. 2118.

Instructions regarding War Diaries and Intelligence Summaries are contained in F. S. Regs., Part II. and the Staff Manual respectively. Title pages will be prepared in manuscript.

Hour, Date, Place	Summary of Events and Information	Remarks and references to Appendices
April 1st 1915 BOESCHEPE	Nothing of importance until	
" 5" " "	15 Territorial NCOs & men of this unit left for England by WO order to return to civil employment with Messrs Ln ERITH KENT.	
" 7" " POPERINGHE	Column moved to billets in farms about 1/3 mile S. of POPERINGHE leaving BOESCHEPE by sections at 1.30 p.m. - 2 p.m. - 2.30 p.m. Hq. retaining in the Town	
" 12" " "	Enemy aircraft dropped bombs, one falling in passing convoy of wagons, killing 4 horses - 1 driver seriously wounded (died next day) & 3 others wounded.	
" 14" " "	Sentries reported Zeppelin airships passed over their lines between 8 & 9 p.m.	
" 24" " "	Hostile shells commenced to fall in the town about 7.30 a.m. at 8.45 a.m. one 5.9 Howr shell fell on Hq. Office destroying it - 2 orderlies slightly wounded - 2 men killed & 2 wounded of ammn-coln.	
	At 9 a.m. - Shell exploded in stables killing 1 & wounding 2. Hq. Charges - no men hurt. Hq. moved to farms 1/2 mile S. of Town.	
" 25" " VLAMERTINGHE	Column moved at 10 a.m. Hq. & main body to VLAMERTINGHE 12.C.27. section in advance at H.11.c.b & H.12.c.b.7.	
" 27" " "	Section in advance, [illegible] to Shelfire, moved to Shelfire.	
" 28" " "	About 4 p.m. - heavy shell fire - moved whole unit to X road H.7.C.4.5 moved on at 6 a.m. to farm H.13.a.3.8. Wagon with explosives hit by Shells near YPRES. 1 driver & 4 mules killed.	
" 30" " "	Observed by enemy aeroplane during morning & shelled from S.E. Commencing at 4.45 p.m. moved to G.23.C.8.2.	

[signature]
LIEUT-COL.,
COMMANDING XXVIIth DIVNL. AMN. COL.

27th Div: Amm'n Col'n
Vol IV 1–31.5.15

Army Form C. 2118.

WAR DIARY
or
INTELLIGENCE SUMMARY
(Erase heading not required.)

Instructions regarding War Diaries and Intelligence Summaries are contained in F. S. Regs, Part II. and the Staff Manual respectively. Title pages will be prepared in manuscript.

Hour, Date, Place	Summary of Events and Information	Remarks and references to Appendices
May 1. Sheet 28 Farm G.21.C.	Nothing to report.	
May 3. " " G.26.C.	Orders received to move to meadow in sheet 28. G. 26. a.	
" 8 G.26.C.	No 2 Section moved up as advanced section to G. 12. d. to facilitate amn. supply.	
about 5. am May 24. "	Heavy calls for gun amn. began to come in.	
8.30 am " " "	Orders to prepare for any eventuality.	
May 25 "	Last call for amn. recd. at 4.45 pm. - In 34 hours the total gunner sent up to the B.des was 12,258 rounds.	
May 26 "	Rations recd. 1 Kat 27th Divn. was transferred to IIIrd Corps.	
night of May 30-31st.	Column moved 19 at midnight to billets near ARMENTIERES where it arrived at 6.30 am. leaving behind No 2 Section	
May. 31st Sheet 36. B.27.C.	(as above) and Hour S/Section of IIIrd Divn Amn. Col. Took over locations occupied by VTR Divl. Amn. Col. - Hour S/Section of Kar unit joined for amn supply duties.	

Francis Somerville
LIEUT-COL,
COMMANDING XXVIIth DIVNL. AMN. COL.

27th Division.

27th Div: Amm" Col"

Vol V June 1915

10/5845

XXVIIth DIVNL AMMN COL.

WAR DIARY
or
INTELLIGENCE SUMMARY

(Erase heading not required.)

Army Form C. 2118.

Instructions regarding War Diaries and Intelligence Summaries are contained in F. S. Regs., Part II. and the Staff Manual respectively. Title pages will be prepared in manuscript.

Hour, Date, Place	Summary of Events and Information	Remarks and references to Appendices
June 1st L'EPINETTE	2nd Section marched in from vicinity of VLAMERTINGHE	
June 15th "	H.Q. moved to Bivouac at HALLOI'BEAU.	
	Otherwise there is nothing to report.	

[signature]
LIEUT-COL,
COMMANDING XXVIIth DIVNL AMN. COL.

3-7-15.

27th Oct: Amm'n Col'n

Army Form C. 2118.

WAR DIARY
or
INTELLIGENCE SUMMARY

(Erase heading not required.)

Instructions regarding War Diaries and Intelligence Summaries are contained in F. S. Regs., Part II. and the Staff Manual respectively. Title pages will be prepared in manuscript.

Hour, Date, Place	Summary of Events and Information	Remarks and references to Appendices
July 1st 1915. Bivouack at l'hallobeau in ARMENTIERES.	Nothing of interest except until :—	
July 15th. La SEQUEMEAU.	Unit moved to la SEQUEMEAU. near CROIX du BAC.	
July 24th. FROID NID.	" " to Bivouacks at FROID NID near STEENWERCK. into winter quarters	

Lucien Brunerie LIEUT-COL,
COMMANDING XXVIIth DIVNL. AMN. COL.

12/7493

29th Division

27th Ammunition Col

Aug - Oct '15

Vol VII

Army Form C. 2118.

WAR DIARY
or
INTELLIGENCE SUMMARY

(Erase heading not required.)

Instructions regarding War Diaries and Intelligence Summaries are contained in F. S. Regs., Part II. and the Staff Manual respectively. Title pages will be prepared in manuscript.

Hour, Date, Place	Summary of Events and Information	Remarks and references to Appendices
1915. August. 1-31. Bivouack near STEENWERCK.	Nothing of interest to report during the month.	
September 6th. "	1st Section placed at disposal of VIIIth B.A.C. in the noon.	
" 7th "	2nd " " " " " " " "	
" 9th "	Mark VII rifles withdrawn replaced with Non Converted pattern rifles MK VI.	
" 14th STEEN-JE	Instructions as under 6th & 7th inst. cancelled. Unit moved	
" 20th "	Complete to STEEN-JE. (nr BAILLEUL.) Marched to HAZEBROUCK, then entraining in 4 Trains at 2½ hr intervals for	
" 21st BLANGY.	LONGEAUX nr AMIENS – 1st train arriving at about midnight. Unit moved out to Bivouack nr. BLANGY–TRONVILLE.	
" 24th BLANGY.	" " to HAMELET.	
" 25th HAMELET.	" " to LE HAMEL – BOUZENCOURT & went into bivouack.	

[signature]
LIEUT-COL.,
COMMANDING XXVIIth DIVNL AMN. COL

Army Form C. 2118.

WAR DIARY
or
INTELLIGENCE SUMMARY
(Erase heading not required.)

Instructions regarding War Diaries and Intelligence Summaries are contained in F. S. Regs., Part II. and the Staff Manual respectively. Title pages will be prepared in manuscript.

Hour, Date, Place		Summary of Events and Information	Remarks and references to Appendices
1915			
October 1st 4 p.m.	HANEL	Unit inspected by Corps Comdr.	
" 12th	"	Orders received to Cpts establishment to that of New Armies.	
" 19th	"	20th Heavy B"y. marched in : were billeted in the Village	
" 23rd	"	Unit marched at 10 a.m. to BOVES. Wire bivouack.	
" 24th	BOVES	" at 9 a.m. via AMIENS to BREILLY, billetted in ruined chateau outside village. H.Q. in Village.	
" 25th to end of month	BREILLY	nothing to report.	

Francis Bonneric
LIEUT-COL.,
COMMANDING XXVIIth DIVNL-AMN. COL

121/7637

27th Dec. Ammsj. ed.

Army Form C. 2118.

WAR DIARY

~~INTELLIGENCE SUMMARY~~

(Erase heading not required.)

Instructions regarding War Diaries and Intelligence Summaries are contained in F. S. Regs., Part II. and the Staff Manual respectively. Title pages will be prepared in manuscript.

Hour, Date, Place	Summary of Events and Information	Remarks and references to Appendices
In the Field 1st to 30th Nov. '15.	In Billets at Breilly during the whole of the month. About the 15th inst, orders were received to re-organise to scale for "SALONIKA FIELD FORCE". All Officers and Men recalled off leave. Mules have now be replaced by L.D. Horses. Orders received to be in readiness to ~~embark~~ entrain for Port of Embarkation at short notice. *[signature]* Lt-Col. In the Field. Commanding 27th Divn Ammtn Colmn. 1st Dec. 1915.	

27 Side Omnris Col.
Doc / vol IX

Army Form C. 2118.

WAR DIARY
or
INTELLIGENCE SUMMARY

(Erase heading not required.)

Instructions regarding War Diaries and Intelligence Summaries are contained in F. S. Regs., Part II. and the Staff Manual respectively. Title pages will be prepared in manuscript.

Hour, Date, Place	Summary of Events and Information	Remarks and references to Appendices
1st to 6th December 1915.	The Column was in Billets at BREILLY-SUR-SOMME.	
7th Dec. 1915.	Column moved to VIGNACOURT.	
7th to 21st December 1915	The Column was in Billets at VIGNACOURT	
23rd Dec.1915.	Column moved to LONGPRE.	
23rd to 31st December 1915.	Column was in Billets at LONGPRE'.	
16th inst, In Action.	Lieut Martin Kirke-Smith. Killed. 811 Gunner Skinner..E. Severely wounded.	Whilst in Command of T.M.B and attached to 99th T.M.B.
In the Field 1st Jany.1916.	*[signature]* Lieut-Col. Commanding 27th Divisional Ammtn Column.	

GS 214

Personnel
Anna Colanna

R.1. 49.   C.217.   .132.

[Stamp: GENERAL STAFF 11 JAN 1915]

Head Quarters,
         27th Division.
----

1.   Ever since the 27th Division left WINCHESTER 3 weeks ago, I have received unsatisfactory reports of the state of the Ammunition Columns of the 1st Brigade and 20th Brigade R.F.A.

2.   I have not reported their condition before, as I considered that both Officers and men, should be allowed time in which to gain experience and show what they were worth.

There is but one Regular Officer in each of the two Columns and the men are Regulars from Reserve Brigades and Territorials mixed.

I have lately received independent and uncalled for reports by the Brigade Commanders in which the state of their Ammunition Columns is reported on in the clearest language.

They do not hesitate to say that, in their present condition, they will prove to be a danger in an emergency.

3.   The Commander of the 1st Brigade Column, Captain J.A.Ballie, R.H.A. (T) is a good officer. He reports that he can get some N.C.O's who can do their work, he cannot be responsible for the consequences.

The O.C. 20th Brigade reports in similar terms, that his N.C.O's, who are Territorials, are quite useless not being able to command men or carry out properly the simplest order.

4.   Further I beg to point out that the Subaltern Officers of these Columns are with one exception, Territorial and Reserve Officers or hold temporary Commissions and cannot be expected to assist in working the Columns as would officers of greater experience or higher training.

5.   If 4 Regular Sergeants can be provided for each Column, I hope to make them efficient.

     The Brigades now under my Command, cannot supply any Sergeants either by promotion or by transfer as they have no suitable men to promote.

6.   Without the assistance I now apply for, I see no hope of efficiency in these units, and I beg that early steps may be taken to supply it.

                    Sd.   A.Stokes, Brig-General,
                        Commanding, 27th Divisional Artillery.

                    -2-   A.133.

Head Quarters,
     2nd Army .

     I entirely agree with the G.O.C. 27th Divisional Artillery, but I doubt if 4 Regular Sergeants for an Ammunition is sufficient.

     I should have thought that more would be required in a unit where a great deal of responsible work and movement of ammunition is being done at night under supervision of N.C.O's.

11th January, 1915.   Sd. T.D'O.Snow, Major General,
                        Commanding, 27th Division.

www.ingramcontent.com/pod-product-compliance
Lightning Source LLC
Chambersburg PA
CBHW081504160426
43193CB00014B/2587